Pigs Never Sweat!

Kelly Tills

Copyright © 2021 Kelly Tills
Paperback Edition

ISBN: 978-1-7367004-1-9

Published by FDI Publishing LLC. All rights reserved. Except for the purposes of fair reviewing, no part of this publication may be reproduced, distributed or transmitted in any form or by any means, or stored in a database or retrieval system, including by any means via the internet, without the prior written permission of the publisher. Infringers of copyright render themselves liable to prosecution.

———————

A division of FDI publishing LLC

The cool thing about pigs is...

pigs never **sweat!**

Dogs and cats sweat through their paws.

People sweat all over.

Horses just sweat a lot.

Does a pig get sweaty when **playing?**

No!
But pigs are very playful.

Does a pig get sweaty
feet? No!
Pigs have hooves.

Does a pig get stinky in the sun?

Yes, but not from sweating!

Sweat

keeps us cool.

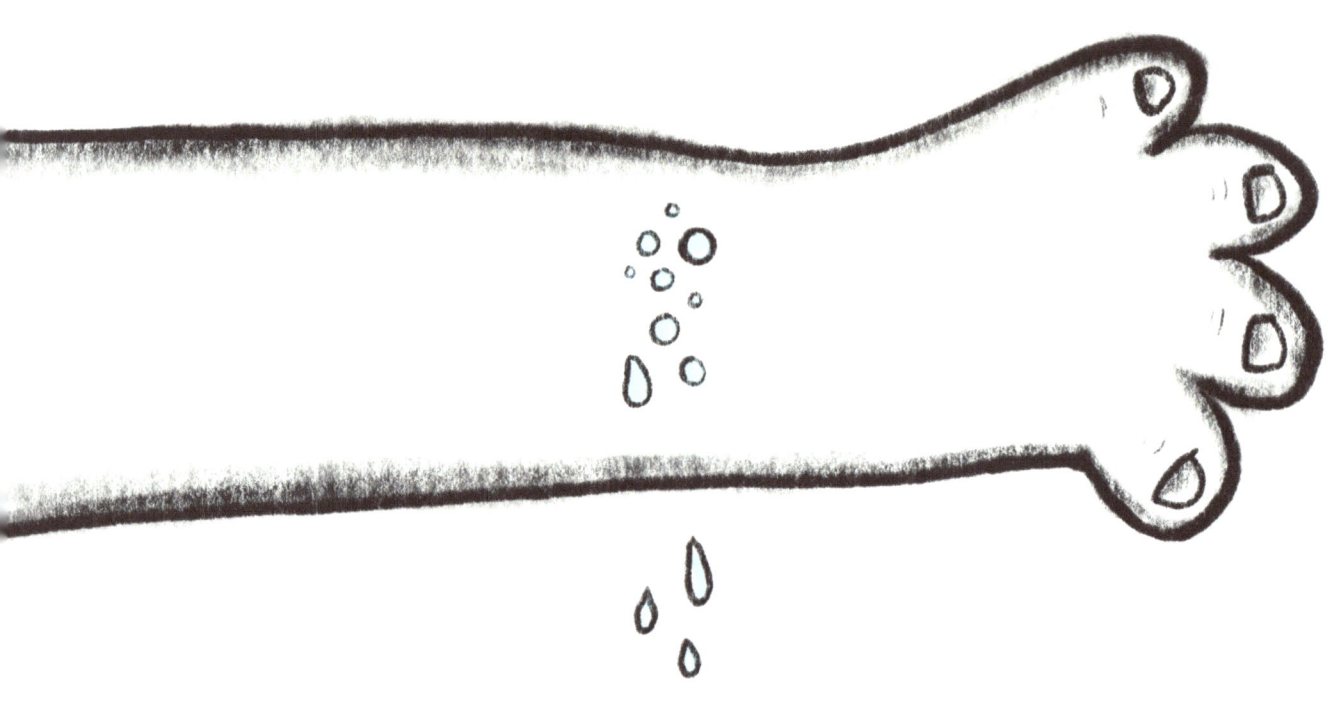

It comes out of our skin in tiny droplets, then it **evaporates** into the air.

Sweating feels so good.

It can also make us stinky.
PEE-YEW!

If pigs never sweat, how do they cool down?

They get muddy!

The mud does not evaporate like sweat. It protects pigs from the sun.

It dries up like a mud jacket and keeps them shady wherever they go.

Can people get muddy too?
That would be very messy.

Mud jackets look better on pigs.

And that's the cool thing about pigs.

Well, actually...

pigs aren't the only mammals that don't sweat. Hippos, rhinos, and marine mammals don't sweat either.

Whoa! That's crazy.

Get More *Awesome Animals* Books

   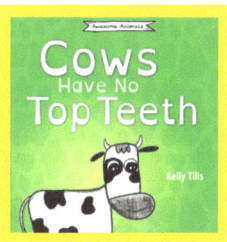 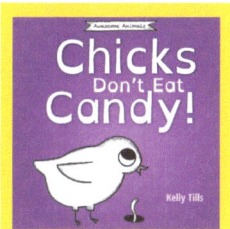

About the Author

Kelly Tills writes silly books for kids and believes even the smallest hat-tip, in the simplest books, can teach our kids how to approach the world. Kelly's children's stories are perfect to read aloud to young children, or to let older kids read themselves (hey, let them flex those new reading skills!). Proud member of the *International Dyslexia Association*.

I hope this book brought you and your tiny human some fun time together. Help others find this book, and experience that same joy by **leaving a review!**

Point your phone's camera here.
It'll take you straight to the review page. Magic!

www.ingramcontent.com/pod-product-compliance
Lightning Source LLC
Chambersburg PA
CBHW050747110526
44590CB00003B/104